This Book Belongs to

*The mission of Storey Communications is to serve our customers
by publishing practical information that encourages personal independence
in harmony with the environment.*

Edited by Pamela Lappies
Cover and interior illustrations by Mary Rich
Cover and text design by Meredith Maker
Text production by Susan Bernier
Indexed by Northwind Editorial Services

Some recipes have been adapted from other Storey/Garden Way Publishing books: pages 10,41: *Herbal Vinegar* by Maggie Oster; pages 12, 34, 46: *The Joy of Gardening* by Janet Ballantyne; pages 18, *Satisfying Soups* by Phyllis Hobson; page 42: *The Busy Person's Guide to Preserving Food* by Janet Chadwick.

For additional information please contact Storey Communications, Inc., Schoolhouse Road, Pownal, Vermont 05261.

Printed in Canada by Métropole Litho

10 9 8 7 6 5 4 3 2 1

Library of Congress
Cataloging-in-Publication Data

Bass, Ruth, 1934–
  Peppers love herbs / Ruth Bass ;
    illustrations by Mary Rich.
      p.   cm.
  "A fresh from the garden cookbook."
  ISBN 0-88266-932-X (hc : alk. paper)
  1. Cookery (Peppers).   2. Cookery
    (Herbs)   I. Title.
TX803.P46B37 1996
641.6'5643—dc20   96-15283
                                    CIP

PEPPERS
LOVE HERBS

A
Fresh from the Garden
Cookbook

RUTH BASS

ILLUSTRATED BY MARY RICH

A Storey Publishing Book
Storey Communications, Inc.

Introduction

Peppers and herbs are best when you fill a basket in the garden, bring them directly to the kitchen, and start cooking. But in most parts of the country, that doesn't work on a twelve-month basis. So you buy them commercially, looking for peppers that have not started to pucker with age or develop a discolored spot that may indicate impending rot, seeking herbs that show no signs of limpness.

These days, peppers abound year-round, big, glossy red and yellow ones from Holland gracing northern markets in the winter, hot ones coming from all sorts of places — some of them stubby, some tiny and blazing hot, some long and green like a witch's fingernail. Sweet peppers can be domineering, and hot peppers shove everything else out of the way unless they're used with discretion. So the trick is to take advantage of their good traits and meld them with herbs that soften their personalities.

Those who dote on food that burns the lips, the mouth, the tastebuds, and even the nostrils sometimes lose sight of the fact that food is supposed to have flavor, not just fire. For those diners, just toss in the hot peppers. But remember that some peppers are much hotter than others: a habanero measures very high on the Richter scale of pepperiness, while the jalapeño is fairly low.

Those who grow peppers have to resist the temptation to douse them with fertilizer. Overfed sweet peppers develop a wonderfully bushy shape and dozens of glossy green leaves. But then they fail to bloom, and all those leaves hide empty branches. Stuff peppers in the kitchen, not in the garden. When you plant hot ones, remember to put them on the other side of the garden. You don't want industrious bees going from hot peppers to sweet ones without intermission — they transfer the heat as they pollinate.

Once you have the peppers in hand, try an assortment of fresh herbs to enhance the sweet ones, temper the hot. A number of them — like chives, oregano, and rosemary — will grow nicely in a perennial garden. Others — like basil, parsley, and dill — need space in a vegetable garden. Those who want to invest large amounts of time in their thyme and sage can design a fancy garden or create a combination of container and garden space against a wall, along a walk, or around a statue or fountain. Herbs are more than tasty. They're pretty. They have foliage in a range of green; they have yellow, purple, white, pink, and lavender flowers; and many of them have added value medicinally or in fragrant potpourris and dried-flower arrangements.

A few hints for using them:

1. Pick herbs early in the morning, after the dew is off but before the sun is high. They will be crisper.
2. Don't spray your herbs with insecticides or herbicides. If you have a problem with them, seek an organic remedy.
3. Wash herbs carefully, and dry them before trying to chop them.
4. If you can't find a fresh herb and must use dried, use half to a third as much. But if you double a recipe, take it easy on the herbs. Doubling *them* may allow them to take over.
5. If you enjoy this collection, exchange a favorite herb for one in a recipe. Most will prove happy combinations.

Jalapeño Pepper Dip

Mix this up several hours ahead of time so that the flavors will have time to seep into every crevice. Then put it in a dip dish and surround it with corn chips, tortilla chips, or slices of zucchini and top with a sprig of parsley. It will *look* bland and harmless. It isn't.

> 1 container (8-ounce) cottage cheese
> 3 garlic cloves, peeled and sliced in half
> 1–2 fresh jalapeño peppers, seeded
> 2 scallions, white part only
> 1 tablespoon fresh parsley, leaves only

1. Scoop the cottage cheese into a blender or food processor and give it a whirl.
2. Add the garlic, jalapeños, scallions, and parsley and process until very smooth.
3. Pour into a serving dish and chill for 3 to 5 hours.

25 SERVINGS
ON CHIPS

Garlicky Bean and Pepper Dip

Refried beans have become a great favorite for hors d'oeuvres. Here's a nonfried bean dip with garlic and cilantro that packs a punch. Remember to handle the jalapeños like the tigers they are.

> 2 tablespoons extra virgin olive oil
> 2 fresh jalapeño peppers, cored, seeded, and minced
> 1 small onion, minced
> 2 garlic cloves, chopped
> 1 can (8-ounce) black beans, drained
> 1 large sweet green pepper, cored, seeded, and chopped
> 2 tablespoons minced fresh cilantro

1. In the order listed, put the olive oil, jalapeños, onion, garlic, black beans, and peppers in a blender or food processor and puree.
2. Pour into a bowl, stir in the cilantro, cover tightly with plastic wrap, and refrigerate for at least 1 hour to allow flavors to blend. Remove 15 minutes before serving. Serve with tortilla chips, corn chips, or celery stalks.

1½ CUPS

Roasted Pepper and Cilantro Butter

For a different spread on crackers — perhaps even crackers you've made yourself — try this pretty butter.

> 4 tablespoons butter, at room temperature
> ½ cup roasted peppers (see instructions, page 45)
> 2 teaspoons hot mustard
> 3 teaspoons chopped fresh cilantro
> Salt and freshly ground pepper

1. In a food processor or blender, cream the butter and gradually add the roasted peppers through the top while it is running.
2. When the butter is rosy red, stop the machine and scrape the sides. Add the mustard and cilantro, process until mixed, and season with salt and pepper to taste.
3. Serve at room temperature.

½ CUP

Red Pepper and Garlic Spread

This garlicky spread can go on crackers, chips, crisp slices of cucumber or zucchini, or rounds of rye bread. But it's best on crostini — thin slices of crusty French bread that you brush on both sides with olive oil and then bake in a hot oven (400°F) for 10 minutes or less.

3 sweet red peppers, roasted and peeled
½ cup extra virgin olive oil
¼ cup pitted and chopped black olives
6 garlic cloves, minced or crushed
2 tablespoons capers
1 tablespoon minced fresh parsley
2 teaspoons lemon juice
Salt and freshly ground black pepper

1. Roast the peppers under the broiler until they are partly charred; place in a plastic bag for 10 minutes. Then peel and dice them.
2. Start with the olive oil, and then add the peppers, olives, garlic, capers, parsley, and lemon juice into a blender or food processor and process for a short time. The mixture should be coarse, not pureed.
3. Let stand at room temperature for at least 1 hour before serving to allow flavors to blend. Add salt and pepper to taste.

2 CUPS

Chili and Cilantro Sambal

For this Indian-style dish, to be used as a condiment with cold meats
or with curry, try those green chili peppers that look like a witch's finger —
long, curved, and talonlike. Respect their hotness. Using a melon baller
is a good way to remove the seeds. If you have a pioneer spirit, spread this
sambal on a turkey or cheese sandwich.

>   6 *fresh green chili peppers, cored, seeded, and minced*
>   1 *cup fresh cilantro*
>   ¼ *cup fresh chives*
> 1½ *slices whole wheat bread, broken into pieces*
>   ¼ *cup lime juice*
>   ⅓ *cup extra virgin olive oil*
>   ½ *inch fresh gingerroot, peeled and minced*
>   ½ *teaspoon cumin*
>   *Salt*

1. Combine chilis, cilantro, chives, bread, lime juice, olive oil, gingerroot,
   and cumin in a food processor or blender and pulse until the ingredients
   have combined but still have texture.
2. Season with salt to taste, and refrigerate for several hours to allow
   flavors to blend. Serve at room temperature.

1 CUP

Green Pepper Jelly with Oregano

Some like it hot, some like it mild — with peppers, you can have it your way. And in fact, if the garden or the roadside stand features more sweet red peppers than green ones, use half and half for a red- and green-pepper jelly.

> 2 cups ground sweet green peppers
> 1 hot pepper (optional)
> 1 tablespoon minced fresh oregano
> I cup white vinegar
> 1 box powdered pectin
> 3½ cups sugar

1. Finely grind the peppers in a hand grinder or food processor.
2. Mix peppers, oregano, vinegar, and pectin in a saucepan and bring to a rolling boil, the kind you can't stir down.
3. Add the sugar and boil hard for 3 minutes, stirring constantly.
4. Pour into clean, hot jelly jars with two-part canning lids, leaving ¼ inch of headroom.
5. Process in boiling water bath for five minutes.

4 HALF PINTS

Pepper Thyme Cheese Bread

You can have your peppers toasted for breakfast, too, with the sweetness of honey and the fragrance of thyme. And if you want to try just a hint of hot, add four or five drops of chili oil to the dough, along with the honey.

2 tablespoons dry yeast
2 tablespoons plus 1 teaspoon honey
4–5 drops chili oil, optional
½ cup lukewarm water
3 tablespoons extra virgin olive oil
1 sweet green pepper, finely chopped
1 sweet red pepper, finely chopped
1 cup milk

1½ teaspoons salt
2 tablespoons minced fresh thyme
3 ounces Monterey Jack cheese, shredded (¾ cup)
3 ounces sharp cheddar cheese, shredded (¾ cup)
2 eggs, beaten, plus 1 egg, beaten
4–4½ cups all-purpose unbleached flour
½ cup wheat bran

1. Combine the yeast, 1 teaspoon of the honey, the chili oil if using, and the water in a small bowl and set aside until the yeast foams.
2. In a medium skillet, heat 1 tablespoon of the olive oil and sauté the peppers until they are limp, 3 to 5 minutes.
3. In a saucepan, combine the milk, the remaining olive oil, and honey. Add the salt, thyme, and cheeses and heat to lukewarm.
4. In a large bowl, combine the peppers, 2 of the beaten eggs, the yeast mixture, and the milk mixture. Stir in 2 cups of the flour. Add the wheat bran and enough additional flour so that the dough begins to pull away from the sides of the bowl.
5. Cover and let the dough rise for 30 minutes. If your house is cold and the dough is sluggish, put a heating pad under it on low or medium. It will perk up.
6. Punch down the dough, divide it in half, and shape each half into a loaf to fit a greased 9-inch loaf pan. Let the bread rise another 30 minutes.
7. Preheat the oven to 375°F. Brush the top of each loaf with the remaining beaten egg, and bake for 30 to 35 minutes.

2 LOAVES

Cornbread with Jalapeños

You can substitute any variety of hot pepper for the jalapeño in this recipe, or change the amount to suit your taste. Handle hot peppers with care: If you get hot pepper juice on your hands and then rub an eye, flush it out with copious amounts of water. The better course is to wear rubber gloves and wash utensils and cutting boards after dealing with these peppers.

½ cup fresh corn kernels or dry-packed canned corn
½ teaspoon salt
1¼ cups low-fat yogurt
½ cup butter, melted, plus more for greasing pan
2 eggs, beaten, or ½ cup cholesterol-free egg substitute
3 tablespoons chopped fresh oregano
3 teaspoons baking powder
1 cup yellow cornmeal
¼ teaspoon white pepper
¼ pound cheddar cheese, shredded
1 jalapeño pepper, cored, seeded, and minced

1. Preheat the oven to 350°F, and butter a 2½-quart casserole dish.
2. In a large bowl, combine the corn kernels, salt, yogurt, melted butter, and eggs or egg product.
3. Combine the oregano, baking powder, cornmeal, and white pepper and stir into the corn and yogurt mixture. Chop the shredded cheese into smaller pieces and fold into the mixture. Add the jalapeño.
4. Pour the batter into the baking dish, and bake for 1 hour. Serve with plenty of butter.

8 SQUARES

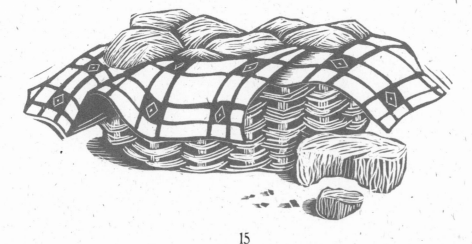

Savory Red Pepper Chowder

You've had chowder with clams, chowder with onions, chowder with fish, and chowder with corn. It's time for chowder with savory and sweet red peppers, picked when they've just turned glossy red and are still crisp.

4 tablespoons butter
2 medium onions, chopped
1 garlic clove, chopped
1 tablespoon minced fresh savory
1 bay leaf, ground with mortar and pestle
½ cup chopped button mushrooms
4 sweet red peppers (3 cups chopped)
Juice of ½ lemon
2 cups chicken broth
3 large potatoes, or enough for 1 cup thinly sliced
4 cups low-fat milk
Salt and freshly ground pepper
¼ cup coarsely chopped fresh parsley

1. In a soup pot, melt the butter and cook the onions gently until they are soft and golden, not browned. After the first 5 minutes, add the garlic, savory, and bay leaf, along with the mushrooms, chopped peppers, and lemon juice. Cook another 5 minutes.

2. Add the broth and sliced potatoes. Simmer, covered, for 25 minutes, or until the potatoes are tender.
3. Add the milk, stir well, and reheat. Add salt and pepper to taste and serve, garnishing with the chopped parsley.

2 QUARTS

Albuquerque Chili with Oregano

Chili con carne, it's called in Mexico; in the United States, the title is more likely to include a hint of fire. Steaming bowls of chili are two-alarm (a little hot), three-alarm (hotter), or four-alarm (conflagration). This one has enough hot chili peppers in it to put it in the four-alarm category for most firefighters.

¼ cup extra virgin olive oil
2 pounds lean beef, cut into ½-inch cubes
2 tablespoons all-purpose unbleached flour
1 medium yellow onion, chopped
2 garlic cloves, chopped
3 large ripe tomatoes, chopped
6–8 small mild chili peppers, seeded and thinly sliced
3 small hot red chili peppers, seeded and thinly sliced,
   or 1 habanero pepper
4 teaspoons minced fresh oregano
½ teaspoon cumin seed
2 cups beef broth
Salt and freshly ground black pepper
4 cups cooked rice

1. In a large skillet, heat 2 tablespoons of the oil and brown the beef. Drain off the fat. Place the beef in a large soup pot.
2. In the same skillet, heat the rest of the oil and blend in the flour, onion, and garlic. Cook until the onion is just starting to brown.
3. Add the onion mixture, tomatoes, chili peppers, oregano, cumin seed, and beef broth to the soup pot. Simmer, covered, for 2 hours, stirring occasionally.
4. Add salt and pepper to taste. Serve in warmed chili bowls over rice or with rice on the side.

4 SERVINGS

Red Pepper Quiche

Even though it's ubiquitous, quiche still sounds exotic, elegant — like something that could be described in the J. Peterman catalog. This quiche is herbed and handsome to boot. What more could you ask of eggs in a pie shell?

1 tablespoon extra virgin olive oil
1 sweet red pepper, finely chopped
8 slices bacon
6 ounces Gruyère cheese, finely shredded (1½ cups)
9-inch unbaked pie shell
3 eggs
1 cup light cream
½ cup low-fat milk
1 tablespoon snipped fresh chives
1 teaspoon minced fresh chervil
Salt and freshly ground pepper
Dash of cayenne

1. In a small skillet, heat the olive oil and gently sauté the chopped pepper until it is soft but not browned. In microwave, cook the bacon between double layers of paper towels for 5 minutes. Change the towels and cook another 2 minutes if bacon isn't crisp. (Or you can cook the bacon the conventional way, in a skillet.) When the bacon slices are no longer hot, crumble them.
2. Preheat the oven to 375°F. Sprinkle the shredded cheese, crumbled bacon, and red pepper evenly over the pie shell.
3. Beat the eggs, cream, and milk until frothy. Add the chives, chervil, salt and pepper to taste, and cayenne, and whisk well. Pour into pie shell.
4. Bake for 45 minutes, or until the quiche is firm and browned. Serve in warm wedges.

6 SERVINGS

*The light purple flowers of chives
make a flavorful addition to salads.*

Pepper Frittata with Dill

Fresh egg whites make not only a satisfying omelette but also a delicious frittata. For brunch, a frittata is more spectacular than scrambled eggs or omelettes. Garlic and dill add zing.

1 tablespoon butter
1 cup chopped onions
1 sweet green pepper, finely chopped
1 sweet red pepper, finely chopped
1 tablespoon snipped fresh dill
2 garlic cloves, minced
Salt and white pepper
6 egg whites
3 slices low-fat cheese, shredded

1. Preheat the broiler in the oven. In a large skillet, melt the butter and slowly cook the onions until they begin to soften, about 10 minutes.
2. Add the peppers, dill, garlic, and salt and pepper to taste to the pan and cook another 5 minutes.
3. In a bowl, beat the egg whites until they are foamy and nearly stiff.

4. Pour the whites over the vegetable mixture, lifting the vegetables so the egg can run underneath. Cook on low heat for 3 to 4 minutes.
5. Place the shredded cheese on top and put the skillet under the broiler for 2 minutes, or until the cheese melts and starts to turn brown.

2–3 SERVINGS

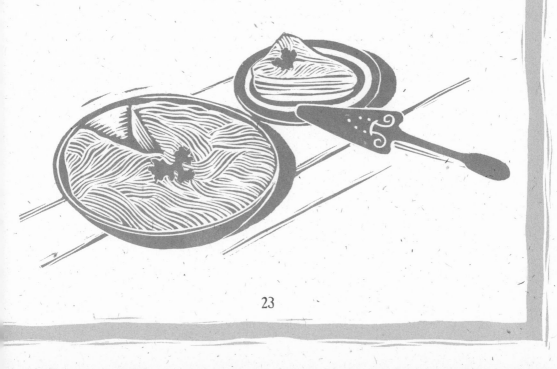

23

Peter Piper's Dill Peppers

If Peter Piper had picked these peppers, he would have gone back for more and more and more. They're sweet. But they're sour. And they're made the day before they're served, so they're easy on the cook.

2 sweet yellow peppers
2 sweet green peppers
1 long English–style cucumber, or 2 regular size
6 young carrots
3 scallions
2 teaspoons salt
4 tablespoons sugar
4 tablespoons white wine vinegar
3 tablespoons snipped fresh dill

1. Slit the peppers lengthwise into strips as thin as possible. If the peppers are very large, cut the strips in half.
2. Cut the cucumber in half lengthwise, remove the seeds with a teaspoon or melon baller, and slice into ¼-inch chunks.
3. Peel the carrots and slice into thin circles.
4. Cut the scallions lengthwise and shred as finely as possible into 2-inch lengths.

5. Put the peppers, cucumber, carrots, and scallions into a large glass bowl and sprinkle the salt over them. Mix and let stand, unrefrigerated, for 3 hours. Drain off the water that is drawn out by the salt.
6. Whisk the sugar and vinegar together. Sprinkle the dill over the salad, add the sugar and vinegar mixture, and toss gently until the dressing is thoroughly mixed through the vegetables. Cover tightly with plastic wrap and refrigerate overnight. Serve chilled.

10 SERVINGS

25

Parsleyed Pepper Pyramid Salad

When peppers are plentiful locally, they make an affordable and handsome salad. In the winter, splurge on those giants from Holland — why doesn't anyone grow them in this country? — and perk up the table with this structure.

2 *large sweet green peppers*
1 *large sweet red pepper*
1 *large sweet yellow or orange pepper*
1 *red onion*
Juice of ½ lemon
4 *tablespoons olive oil*
⅛ *teaspoon cayenne*
1 *teaspoon cumin*
Large bunch of light-green oak-leaf lettuce,
    or 3 heads bibb lettuce
12–15 *pitted black olives*
Freshly ground black pepper
¼ *cup chopped fresh parsley*

1. Leaving the cores in for stability, slice the 4 peppers into thin rings, trying not to break any of them. Discard the core end.
2. Slice the onion thinly.

3. Whisk together the lemon juice, oil, cayenne, and cumin.
4. Mound the lettuce leaves on a large glass plate, piling them higher in the center. Circle the outside of the plate with a row of onion slices. Place green pepper rings on top of the onions, followed by a row of red pepper rings slightly overlapping the green ones. Working toward the center, add another row of green rings, then a row of the yellow or orange, then another red. Repeat, with the circles getting smaller and smaller, until you have used up the peppers and created a pyramid of salad.
5. Arrange the black olives on the salad. Pour the dressing over the top, grind black pepper to taste over the pyramid, and sprinkle with the parsley.

6 SERVINGS

27

Arranged Pepper Salad

Chinese and Japanese dishes are often tossed in a wok, but other times the various ingredients are carefully arranged as if they were flowers or sweets. This salad tastes good and also looks beautiful. Triple it, and make it an edible decoration on a buffet.

2 tablespoons light soy sauce
1 teaspoon sugar
1 garlic clove, pressed
2 tablespoons chopped fresh chervil
5 tablespoons extra virgin olive oil
2 tablespoons white wine vinegar
1 cup torn leaf lettuce
½ cup torn spinach leaves
½ cup finely shredded cabbage
1 cup fresh bean sprouts
1 cup thinly sliced button mushrooms
1 sweet green pepper, sliced in thin strips
1 sweet banana pepper, or other yellow pepper, sliced in thin strips

1. Whisk together the soy sauce, sugar, garlic clove, chervil, olive oil, and vinegar. Set aside so the flavors have a chance to blend.

2. Toss the lettuce, spinach, and cabbage together and circle the outside of a shallow bowl with the mixture.

3. Mound the bean sprouts in the center and arrange the mushroom slices around them, overlapping each slice with the next. Make decorative X's with green and yellow pepper strips on the bean sprouts.

4. Drizzle the dressing over all.

4 SERVINGS

29

Grilled Salad with Herbs

Here's a salad that can be served warm, not-so-warm, or even chilled if you want to wait awhile. While grilling lamb chops or chicken, add some vegetables to the fire: red, green, and yellow peppers, a small eggplant — or whatever is available — Spanish onions, a couple of leeks.

1 sweet red pepper
1 sweet green pepper
1 sweet yellow pepper
1 small eggplant
1 Spanish onion
2 large leeks, split lengthwise and rinsed carefully
2 garlic cloves, minced
1 tablespoon chopped fresh oregano
1 tablespoon chopped fresh parsley
1½ tablespoons balsamic vinegar
¼ cup extra virgin olive oil
½ teaspoon dry mustard
Salt and freshly ground pepper
12 cherry tomatoes

1. Put the peppers, eggplant, onion, and leeks on the grill and let them cook until charred, turning occasionally. You may need a piece of screening or a slab of slate over the grate so the vegetables won't fall into the fire.
2. While the vegetables are cooking, combine the garlic, oregano, parsley, vinegar, oil, dry mustard, and salt and pepper to taste in a jar with a tightly fitting lid. Shake well and set aside to let the flavors blend.
3. When the vegetables are well cooked, remove from the grill, peel, and chop coarsely. Place in an attractive salad bowl and either chill for 1 hour or serve warm with the dressing. Garnish with the tomatoes.

4 TO 6 SERVINGS

Herbed Peppers and Oranges

Human minds are filled with color codes, so color — consciously or unconsciously — affects how people feel about food. That's why you just can't plop a chicken breast, a mound of mashed potatoes, and a pile of cauliflower on a plate. This salad, for color and taste, is an attention getter.

3 sweet green peppers, cored and seeded
2 oranges, with the zest removed from one and reserved
2 heads Boston or bibb lettuce
4 cups torn spinach leaves, with tough stems removed
3 tablespoons extra virgin olive oil
1 tablespoon balsamic vinegar
2 teaspoons lemon verbena, minced
¼ teaspoon sugar
Zest of 1 orange
Salt and freshly ground black pepper
1 red onion, sliced in paper-thin rings
¼ cup farmer cheese

1. Slice the peppers into long thin strips. Cut the oranges in half as you would a grapefruit, and scoop out the sections with a grapefruit spoon.

2. Toss the lettuce and spinach together and mound on a large white or clear-glass plate.
3. Make the dressing, whisking together the oil, vinegar, lemon verbena, sugar, orange zest, and salt and pepper to taste.
4. Arrange the pepper slices, orange sections, and onion rings on top of the lettuce in a decorative way. Scatter crumbled farmer cheese over the top, and drizzle the dressing over the whole salad.

6 SERVINGS

Savory Shrimp and Pepper Salad

Summertime, and the living is supposed to be easier. Take some garden peppers and onions and herbs, cook up some shrimp and pasta, and have dinner ready before lunch and the heat of the day.

½ *pound rotini or elbow pasta*
1 *cup water*
Juice of 1 lemon
1 *pound uncooked shrimp*
1 *large sweet red or orange pepper, chopped*
1 *tablespoon minced red onion*
2 *tablespoons minced fresh parsley*
4 *tablespoons crumbled feta cheese*
½ *cup extra virgin olive oil*
1 *tablespoon Balsamic vinegar*
1 *garlic clove, minced*
1 *tablespoon minced fresh savory*
¼ *teaspoon white pepper*
Salt

1. In a large saucepan, bring 4 quarts of water to a boil and cook the pasta until it is just tender. Drain, flush with cold water, and drain again.
2. In a saucepan, bring the water and 1 tablespoon of the lemon juice to a boil. Add the shrimp and simmer for 3 to 5 minutes. Drain, shell, and devein.
3. Combine the pasta, shrimp, pepper, onion, parsley, and feta cheese in a large salad bowl.
4. Combine the oil, vinegar, garlic, savory, pepper, and salt to taste in a jar with a tightly fitting lid, and shake to blend. Pour over the salad and toss to coat. Chill for at least 1 hour before serving.

SERVES 4–6

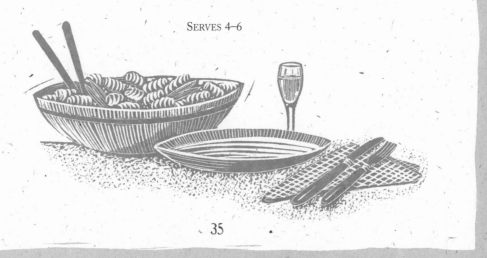

Steamed Peppers with Black Olives

Most pepper recipes find the peppers surrounded by other vegetables or meats. This one surrounds them with fresh herbs to let the peppers shine.

> 2 large sweet green peppers
> 2 large sweet red or orange peppers
> 3 tablespoons extra virgin olive oil
> 2 garlic cloves, minced or pressed
> 2 onions, minced
> 1 tablespoon finely chopped fresh, oregano
> 1 tablespoon finely chopped fresh, parsley
> 1 teaspoon finely chopped fresh, rosemary
> 1½ teaspoons ground cumin
> ½ jalapeño pepper, cored, seeded, and minced
> Salt and freshly ground pepper
> 12 pitted black olives, coarsely chopped
> 1 tablespoon capers

1. Wash the peppers, pat them dry, and cut them in half. Remove the seeds and membranes and slice lengthwise into 6 strips per pepper.
2. In a large skillet, heat the oil and add the pepper strips, skin side down.

3. Sprinkle the garlic and onions over the top, then the oregano, parsley, rosemary, cumin, jalapeño, and salt and pepper to taste. Toss and stir to lightly coat everything with the oil, adding another teaspoon or two of oil if necessary.

4. Cover and cook over medium heat until the onions and peppers are tender but not mushy, about 15 minutes. Add the black olives and capers and toss again. Cook another 5 minutes without covering.

8 SERVINGS

Stir-Fried Peppers with Parsley

The Chinese get the wok very hot, add a small amount of oil, then put in various flavorings and the freshest of vegetables and toss them about rapidly for a very short time. The result comes in way ahead of boiling.

1 tablespoon cornstarch
1 tablespoon cold water
2 tablespoons peanut oil
1 tablespoon sesame seed oil
2 tablespoons shredded hot red pepper
1 tablespoon black bean sauce
3 garlic cloves, minced
2 large sweet green peppers, cored, seeded, and cut into ¼-inch strips
4 large carrots, peeled and shredded
¼ pound fresh bean sprouts
¼ cup chicken broth
¼ cup sherry or rice wine
3 scallions, green and white parts, shredded
¼ cup chopped fresh parsley

1. Dissolve the cornstarch in the water and set aside.
2. Heat a wok or large skillet until a drop of water skitters around the pan. Add the peanut and sesame oils and swirl to coat the pan. Stir in the hot pepper, black bean sauce, and garlic. Scoop and turn the mixture for 1 minute.
3. Add the sweet peppers, carrots, and bean sprouts, continuing to scoop and turn the vegetables rapidly for about 1 minute. Stir in the chicken broth and sherry or wine, and heat to boiling.
4. Stir in the cornstarch mixture and stir about 20 seconds, or until thickened. Add the scallions and parsley. Cook and stir for 30 seconds. Serve as hot as possible.

4–6 SERVINGS

Potatoes and Peppers

Basically, these potatoes and peppers are steamed. The potatoes may get a little brown, but it's fine if they stay white. The object is to cook them so slowly that they get soft gradually and absorb the taste of onions, garlic, and peppers. An electric skillet works well for this dish because the heat can be regulated precisely.

   10 large potatoes
    5 tablespoons extra virgin olive oil
    1 onion, finely chopped
    5 garlic cloves, chopped
    2 large sweet green peppers, chopped
   ½ cup chopped fresh parsley

1. Peel the potatoes, cut into ½-inch cubes, and leave in cold water until it is time to cook them.
2. In a deep skillet that has a cover, heat the oil and cook the onion and garlic slowly for about 5 minutes. Add the peppers. Drain the potatoes and add them. Stir.
3. Turn the heat almost to low and cook 1–1½ hours. A few minutes before serving, stir in the chopped parsley.

8–10 SERVINGS

40

Almond Pepper Sauce

A Spanish sauce made with some sweet and some hot peppers can be used on fresh grilled tuna steaks or swordfish or on steamed vegetables. A tablespoonful or two could easily be added to a seafood soup or stew.

1 cup blanched, slivered almonds
2 hard-cooked egg yolks
1 sweet red pepper, roasted, peeled, cored, and seeded
1 fresh habanero or other hot red pepper
2 garlic cloves, chopped
¼ cup chopped fresh parsley
1 tablespoon chopped fresh cilantro
¼ cup white wine vinegar
¾ cup extra virgin olive oil
3 tablespoons boiling water

1. Combine almonds, egg yolks, sweet and hot peppers, garlic, parsley, cilantro, and vinegar in a food processor or blender. Process until smooth.
2. With the machine running, slowly add the olive oil and then the boiling water. Store in a glass container and refrigerate until needed.

2 CUPS

Peppers Stuffed with Herbed Cheese

Even if you're a dedicated carnivore, you can make a meal out of these hearty cheese-crammed peppers. Try them hot with an all-green salad with citrus dressing on the side. They can be made with red, green, or orange peppers.

> 4 large sweet peppers
> 1 large tomato, peeled
> 1 tablespoon chopped fresh basil
> 1 teaspoon snipped fresh chives
> ½ teaspoon Worcestershire sauce
> Salt and white pepper
> ½ pound sharp cheddar cheese cut into ¼-inch cubes
> ½ pound Swiss cheese, cut into ¼-inch cubes

1. Preheat the oven to 375°F, and grease a baking dish large enough to hold the peppers upright.
2. Slice the stem end off the peppers, and carefully remove the seeds and membranes.
3. Bring about 2 inches of water to a boil in a large kettle, stand the peppers in the kettle, and cook for about 6 minutes.
4. Remove the peppers and place in the baking dish. Drop the tomato into the hot water for 30 seconds, remove, peel, and chop.

5. Combine the tomato, basil, chives, Worcestershire sauce, and salt and pepper to taste, and spoon into the peppers.
6. Mix the two cheeses together and add to the peppers, rounding off the tops. The peppers should be stuffed full.
7. Bake for at least 20 minutes, until the peppers are hot and the cheese is melted.

SERVES 4

Dilly Yellow Peppers and Beans

Put olives, garlic, and anchovies together, and you start thinking of the south of France, where vegetables reign supreme. If you can't find yellow peppers, use red. If you can't find red, use green.

4 sweet yellow peppers, sliced
    lengthwise and seeded
2 tablespoons extra virgin olive oil
1 yellow onion, finely chopped
3 garlic cloves, minced
¼ cup chopped fresh parsley

2 tablespoons snipped fresh dill
1 can (16-ounce) black beans
1 can anchovies, drained and mashed
¼ cup dry white wine
12–15 Greek olives, pitted and chopped
    Freshly ground black pepper

1. Blanch the pepper halves in boiling water for 3 to 5 minutes. Drain, run cool water over the peppers, and drain again.
2. In a medium-size skillet, heat the oil and cook the onion for 5 minutes. Add the garlic and cook another 5 minutes, or until the onion is translucent but not browned. Stir in the parsley and dill.
3. Preheat the oven to 350°F. Transfer the onion mixture to a bowl. Add the black beans, anchovies, wine, olives, and black pepper to taste. Fill the pepper halves with the mixture, and place them in a baking dish with about 3 tablespoons of water in the bottom. Cover and bake for 20 minutes.

4–6 SERVINGS

Red Pepper Sauce with Fish

Roasted peppers are a simple dish — and a delicacy. After roasting, a pepper can be used in any number of ways. Here, roasted peppers blended with basil and parsley become a sauce for fish.

4 small sweet red peppers
1 cup chicken broth
½ cup dry white wine
1 garlic clove, minced
1 tablespoon chopped fresh basil

2 tablespoons chopped fresh parsley
½ teaspoon turmeric
1 tablespoon butter
Grilled or poached fish
Lemon wedges

1. To roast peppers, place them in a baking dish and bake uncovered on the lowest rack in the oven at 450°F for 30 minutes, or until they are blackened on all sides. Turn 3 or 4 times during the roasting. When they are done, place them in a paper bag and roll the top closed. Leave for 10 minutes. Take them out and peel.
2. Put peeled peppers, broth, wine, and garlic in a blender and puree.
3. Pour the mixture into a medium skillet; add the basil, parsley, and turmeric and cook slowly until the sauce has thickened. Add the butter and reheat until the butter is melted. Make a circle of sauce on each individual plate and place a piece of grilled or poached fish on it. Top with a lemon wedge for garnish.

ABOUT 1 CUP

45

Herbed Pepper Calzones

Basically, a calzone is a cross between a folded-up pizza and a turnover. If you've never had one, this mix of peppers, herbs, and cheese is a good place to start.

1 tablespoon yeast
1⅓ cups warm water
2 tablespoons canola oil
Pinch of sugar
1 teaspoon salt
4 cups all-purpose unbleached flour
3 Italian hot sausages
3 sweet turkey sausages
2 large onions, diced
1 garlic clove, minced
1 tablespoon minced fresh marjoram

2 teaspoons minced fresh thyme
3 sweet green peppers, cored, seeded, and sliced into thin strips
3–5 tablespoons olive oil
2 cups chopped shiitake mushrooms
½ cup chopped black olives
1½ cups shredded mozzarella cheese
¼ cup grated Parmesan cheese
¼ cup grated Romano cheese
1 egg
4 cups heated tomato sauce (optional)

1. Combine the yeast, water, canola oil, and sugar in a bowl and let stand until the yeast foams. Add the salt and 2 cups of the flour, and beat the dough until it is elastic and smooth. Then stir in the remaining 2 cups of flour.

2. Knead the dough for about 10 minutes, adding flour if necessary. Cover with a damp towel or plastic wrap and set in a warm place for about 45 minutes. It should double in size.

3. Remove the casings from both kinds of sausages, and then crumble the sausage into a large skillet. Fry, continuing to break up the sausage into fine pieces. Remove the meat to a large bowl, drain off all but 2 tablespoons of the fat, and add the onions, garlic, marjoram, thyme, and peppers. If there is no fat, add 2 tablespoons of the olive oil.

4. Cook the onions and peppers until soft and add to the sausage. Heat 3 tablespoons of olive oil in the same pan and cook the mushrooms until they are soft, about 5 minutes. Add them to the vegetables and sausage. Stir in the cheeses.

5. Preheat the oven to 375°F, and grease a cookie sheet.

6. When the dough has risen, punch it down and divide into 8 chunks. Form each chunk into a ball and, on a lightly floured board, roll each into an 8-inch circle. Spoon ⅛ of the filling onto each circle, brush the edges of the dough with water, fold in half, and crimp the edges.

7. Place the calzones on the cookie sheet and let rise, covered with a damp towel, for about 20 minutes. Beat the egg and brush it on the top of the calzones. Bake for 35 minutes. Serve hot as is or with tomato sauce.

8 SERVINGS

47

Peppers and Sun-Dried Tomatoes with Pasta

Pasta, homemade or store-bought, is always available. When vegetables are at their prime, they toss well with pasta — any or all of them. Try this one with sweet peppers, hot sausage, and herbs, a sort of distant cousin of carbonara. Eat it with spaghetti or linguini.

> 4 sweet red bell peppers
> 4 tablespoons olive oil
> 2 Italian sausages, hot or sweet
> 4 garlic cloves, peeled and sliced in half
> 1 pound spaghetti or linguini
> 2 tablespoons sun-dried tomatoes packed in oil, drained and chopped
> 3 tablespoons grated Romano cheese
> ¾ cup grated Parmesan cheese
> 3 tablespoons chopped fresh basil
> 3 tablespoons chopped fresh parsley
> 2 scallions, green and white parts, shredded

1. Roast the peppers in a baking pan, uncovered, on the lowest rack in the oven at 450°F for about 30 minutes, or until they are blackened on all sides.

Turn 3 or 4 times during the roasting. When they are done, place them in a paper bag and roll the top closed. Leave for 10 minutes. When you take them out, peel and let cool. Chop them coarsely.

2. In a skillet, heat the oil. Remove the casings from the sausages and crumble the sausages into the pan. Add the garlic and cook, continuing to separate the sausage meat into crumb-size pieces until they are brown and crisp. Remove the garlic and discard.

3. In the meantime, bring a large pot of water to a boil, and cook the spaghetti or liguini.

4. Combine the warm peppers, sausage, and sun-dried tomatoes. In a separate bowl, combine the Romano and ½ cup of the Parmesan with the , basil, parsley, and scallions. When the pasta is cooked, drain it quickly and place in a large pasta bowl. Cover with the pepper mixture, then the cheese and herb mixture, and toss. Serve at once with the remaining cheese.

4 SERVINGS

Tarragon Chicken and Sweet Peppers

Certain baseball players, heart patients, semivegetarians, and the cholesterol conscious all have a basic fear: They eat so much chicken every year that they're afraid they may wake up squawking one morning. Perhaps they will, but they don't need to be bored. Chicken can be made more ways than there are days in the year, enhanced by almost any herb in the garden.

3 chicken breasts, boned, skinned, and halved
¼ cup unbleached flour
2 tablespoons minced fresh tarragon
Salt and freshly ground pepper
3 tablespoons extra virgin olive oil
1 large sweet onion, diced
2 sweet green peppers, cored, seeded, and cut in strips
I cup dry white wine
1 tablespoon soy sauce
1 cup seedless white grapes

1. Pound the chicken breasts between layers of wax paper until they are fairly thin. Dredge the chicken breasts in the flour, tarragon, and salt and pepper to taste.

2. Heat the oil in a large skillet and add the chicken, turning quickly to brown on both sides. Remove the chicken with a Chinese strainer or slotted spoon and place in a shallow baking dish.
3. Preheat the oven to 375°F. Add the onion and peppers to the skillet and cook slowly until tender. Add the wine and soy sauce, heat to boiling, and cook for another minute. Pour the sauce over the chicken. Cover the baking dish and bake for 12 minutes.
4. In the meantime, slice the grapes in half. When the chicken is ready, add the grapes and bake another 5 to 6 minutes.

4–6 SERVINGS

Stuffed Peppers with Basil

When the sweet green peppers are fat, juicy, and still crisp, find eight that will make nice boats when they're sliced in half lengthwise. These are just right for stuffing, and half the batch can be frozen for another day. Hint: Watch out for the chili powder — it likes to stick to the pan.

1 pound very lean ground beef
2 large onions, chopped
1 garlic clove, minced
2 tablespoons chopped fresh basil
1 jalapeño pepper, seeded and minced
2 teaspoons chili powder
Salt and freshly ground black pepper
2 cups tomato puree
2 tablespoons sugar
1 tablespoon soy sauce
¼ cup low-fat milk
½ pound sharp cheddar cheese, shredded
1½ cups cooked rice
¼ cup chopped fresh parsley
8 sweet green peppers

1. In a large skillet or saucepan, cook the beef, onions, and garlic until the meat is browned.
2. Add the basil, jalapeño pepper, chili powder, and salt and pepper to taste, stirring well. Combine the tomato puree, sugar, soy sauce, and milk and add to the skillet. Bring to a simmer, cover, and cook for 10 minutes.
3. Stir in the shredded cheese and cook over low heat, stirring until the cheese has melted. Stir in the rice and parsley, and remove from heat. Set aside to cool.
4. In the meantime, bring to a boil in a large pot enough water to cover the peppers. Preheat the oven to 400°F. Cut the peppers lengthwise, removing the seeds, stems, and the membranes. Drop into boiling water for about 3 minutes. Drain and cool.
5. Stuff the peppers with the rice mixture. Place peppers on a cookie sheet or in a shallow baking dish. Cover and bake for 30 minutes.
6. To freeze, place peppers on a cookie sheet and put them in the freezer. When they are frozen, wrap, seal, label, and store them in the freezer. To serve from the freezer, partially thaw the peppers in the refrigerator and bake for 45 minutes.

8 SERVINGS

Chinese Pepper Beef

Black beans and peppers contribute distinctive flavors to this beef dish, which can be made either in a wok or a large skillet. Like many Chinese recipes, it looks forbidding because it has so many ingredients. But once the cutting and chopping has been done, much of it ahead of time, the cooking time is short.

STIR-FRY INGREDIENTS
- 1 pound lean sirloin tips or filet of beef
- 2 sweet green peppers
- 1 sweet red or yellow pepper
- 6 garlic cloves
- 3 scallions
- 1 fresh hot red chili pepper or 3 dried hunan chilies
- 1 teaspoon cornstarch
- 6 tablespoons water
- 5 tablespoons peanut oil
- Salt and freshly ground black pepper
- 2½ tablespoons black bean paste
- 1 tablespoon sherry or rice wine
- ¼ cup finely chopped fresh parsley

MARINADE INGREDIENTS
- ¼ teaspoon salt
- ¼ teaspoon sugar
- 2 teaspoons light soy sauce
- ¼ teaspoon freshly ground pepper
- 2 teaspoons sherry
- 1½ teaspoons cornstarch
- 3 tablespoons water
- 1 teaspoon peanut oil
- 1 teaspoon Asian sesame oil

1. With a sharp knife, slice the beef across the grain into pieces about an inch wide, 1½-inches long and ¼-inch thick. Put into a large glass bowl.

54

2. To make the marinade, combine the salt, sugar, soy sauce, pepper, and sherry and pour over the meat.
3. Dissolve the cornstarch in the 3 tablespoons of water. Add to the meat mixture gradually while turning the meat. Add the two oils and turn again. Cover tightly and refrigerate for a t least 30 minutes and up to 2 hours.
4. In the meantime, core, halve, and seed the sweet green and red peppers, and cut them into thin slices, lengthwise. Peel and mince or press the garlic. Clean and cut the scallions into 1-inch pieces, separating the white part from the green. Core, seed, and finely chop the hot pepper, being careful not to get the juice on your hands or in your eyes. In a small bowl, dissolve the cornstarch in the 6 tablespoons of water.
5. When the marinating time is up, heat 1 tablespoon of the peanut oil in a pre-heated skillet or wok, swirl the oil around, add the sweet peppers, and stir-fry for about 2 minutes, keeping the vegetables moving constantly. Season with salt and pepper to taste and remove to a warm plate.
6. Reheat the wok or skillet, add the rest of the oil, and swirl it around. Add the garlic and white part of the scallions. Keep stirring.
7. Add the black bean paste and the hot pepper. Stir in the beef with any remaining marinade and stir and toss until the beef is partially cooked.
8. Splash the sherry into the pan and continue to stir and toss the meat. Add the dissolved cornstarch, sweet peppers, and green part of the scallions. Mix until the sauce has thickened and the beef is done, perhaps another 2 minutes. Serve immediately.

2 SERVINGS IF USED ALONE, 4 IF OTHER MAIN DISHES ARE PREPARED

Venison and Peppers with Savory

Our friend Gary doesn't come home from the hunt empty-handed as a rule. So when it's deer season, his success nets a fair amount of venison. This recipe with peppers and savory is a delicious approach, and for those who don't care for venison, it's easy enough to substitute beef.

> 1 pound of venison round steak or other steak
> 1 tablespoon cornstarch
> 1 teaspoon sugar
> ½ inch gingerroot, peeled and shredded
> 2–3 tablespoons light soy sauce
> 1½ tablespoons dry sherry or dandelion wine
> 2 medium or 3 small sweet green or red peppers
> 4 tablespoons extra virgin olive oil
> ½ teaspoon salt
> 1 garlic clove, crushed
> 2 tablespoons minced fresh savory
> 2 cups cooked rice

1. Cut venison across the grain into slices about 2-inches long and ¼-inch thick.
2. Combine cornstarch, sugar, and gingerroot, and blend in the soy sauce and sherry or wine. Toss with the sliced venison in a large glass or ceramic bowl and set aside.
3. Cut the peppers into 1½-inch pieces. Pour 2 tablespoons of the oil into a large skillet over high heat. Add the salt, then the peppers, and cook, stirring constantly, until the peppers turn a deeper color, about 1 minute.
4. Remove the peppers, leaving the oil. Add the remaining oil, garlic, and savory, and stir in the venison mixture. Cook for 2 minutes, or until venison is done.
5. Add the peppers to the pan, mix well, heat through, and serve immediately with rice. Add more sherry or wine if you want more sauce.

4 SERVINGS

Scallopini with Peppers
and Shiitake Mushrooms

The veal must be pale and pounded thin. The peppers should be freshly picked and crisp. The mushrooms should be perky, not tired. Then the dish will melt in your mouth.

8 *veal scallopini, pounded thin*
4 *tablespoons extra virgin olive oil*
¼ *cup flour*
4 *tablespoons butter*
2 *sweet green peppers, cored, seeded, and sliced into very thin strips*
8 *shiitake mushrooms, cleaned and sliced*
¼ *cup chopped fresh parsley*
2 *teaspoons chopped fresh sage*
Salt and freshly ground pepper
Juice of 1 lemon
½ *cup dry white wine*
Rice or pasta

1. If the scallopini are not well pounded, pound them some more between two sheets of wax paper.
2. Heat the oil in a large skillet. Dredge the scallopini in the flour, shaking off the excess, and cook them in a single layer, browning quickly, possibly only 1 minute per side. Remove to a warm platter as they are done.
3. Drain the oil from the pan, but do not clean it. Add the butter, and when it has melted, slowly sauté the peppers and mushrooms. After about 5 minutes, stir in the parsley, sage, and salt and pepper to taste. Add the lemon juice and continue to cook for another 1–2 minutes.
4. Add the scallopini to the skillet and scoop the sauce over them, turning them until they are coated. Add the white wine and continue the slow cooking until peppers, mushrooms, veal, and sauce are hot. Serve immediately with rice or pasta.

6 SERVINGS

Pork and Peppers Oriental

The Chinese are magical with pork in many forms, and this recipe has more than a hint of Asian cuisine in its flavorings. And like many Chinese dishes it cooks so quickly that it's the perfect answer for a two-career family. Fluffy rice and a tossed salad complete the meal.

2   *pounds pork loin, lean and boneless*
2   *garlic cloves, chopped*
¼   *cup light soy sauce*
2   *teaspoons cornstarch*
3   *tablespoons water*
4   *tablespoons safflower oil*
1   *large onion, cut into eighths*
1   *sweet red pepper, cut into strips*
1   *sweet yellow pepper, cut into strips*
2   *sweet green peppers, cut into strips*
2   *medium hot chili peppers, seeded and chopped*
1   *inch gingerroot, peeled and shredded*
½   *cup chopped fresh parsley*
1   *tablespoon sesame oil*
2   *teaspoons rice wine vinegar*
2   *tablespoons sugar*

1. Slice the pork into ¼-inch-thick slices, stack several slices at once, and cut into thin strips. In a bowl, combine the strips with the garlic and soy sauce. Dissolve the cornstarch in the water, pour over pork, and toss to coat the pieces. Set aside.
2. In a large skillet, heat the safflower oil until it is quite hot. Remove the pork strips from the marinade (reserving the leftover marinade) and add to the skillet, stirring while the meat browns and cooks, about 5 minutes. Remove the pork to a platter.
3. Add to the bowl with the remaining marinade the gingerroot, parsley, sesame oil, vinegar, and sugar. Stir with a fork until blended.
4. Add the onion, sweet peppers, and chili peppers to the skillet. Cook for 3 minutes. The peppers will be tender but not soft.
5. Return the pork to the skillet, along with the contents of the bowl. Bring the mixture to a boil. Let it boil for 1 minute, then reduce the heat and simmer for 2 minutes. The onions should still be crisp.

6 SERVINGS

Index

Converting Recipe Measurements to Metric

Use the following formulas for converting U.S. measurements to metric. Since the conversions are not exact, it's important to convert the measurements for all of the ingredients to maintain the same proportions as the original recipe.

WHEN THE MEASUREMENT GIVEN IS	MULTIPLY IT BY	TO CONVERT TO
teaspoons	4.93	milliliters
tablespoons	14.79	milliliters
fluid ounces	29.57	milliliters
cups (liquid)	236.59	milliliters
cups (liquid)	.236	liters
cups (dry)	275.31	milliliters
cups (dry)	.275	liters
pints (liquid)	473.18	milliliters
pints (liquid)	.473	liters
pints (dry)	550.61	milliliters
pints (dry)	.551	liters
quarts (liquid)	946.36	milliliters
quarts (liquid)	.946	liters
quarts (dry)	1101.22	milliliters
quarts (dry)	1.101	liters
gallons	3.785	liters
ounces	28.35	grams
pounds	.454	kilograms
inches	2.54	centimeters
degrees Fahrenheit	$\frac{5}{9}$ (temperature − 32)	degrees Celsius

While standard metric measurements for dry ingredients are given as units of mass, U.S. measurements are given as units of volume. Therefore, the conversions listed above for dry ingredients are given in the metric equivalent of volume.